W9-AUI-780

ORANGE COUNTY
HIGH SCHOOL LIBRARY

Popular Rock Superstars of Yesterday and Today
POP ROCK

AC/DC

Aerosmith

The Allman
Brothers Band

The Beatles

Billy Joel

Bob Marley
and the Wailers

Bruce Springsteen

The Doors

Elton John

The Grateful Dead

Led Zeppelin

Lynyrd Skynyrd

Pink Floyd

Queen

The Rolling
Stones

U2

The Who

The Who

Noa Flynn

Mason Crest Publishers

The Who

FRONTIS The Who—(left to right) Keith Moon, John Entwistle, Pete Townshend, and Roger Daltrey—are considered by many to be one of the greatest bands of all time.

Produced by 21st Century Publishing and Communications, Inc.

Editorial by Harding House Publishing Services, Inc.

Copyright © 2008 by Mason Crest Publishers. All rights reserved. No part of this publication may be reproduced or transmitted in any form or by any means, electronic or mechanical, including photocopying, recording, taping, or any information storage and retrieval system, without permission from the publisher.

MASON CREST PUBLISHERS INC.
370 Reed Road
Broomall, Pennsylvania 19008
(866) MCP-BOOK (toll free)
www.masoncrest.com

Printed in the United States.

First Printing

9 8 7 6 5 4 3 2 1

Library of Congress Cataloging-in-Publication Data

Flynn, Noa.
   The Who / Noa Flynn.
     p. cm. — (Popular rock superstars of yesterday and today)
   Includes bibliographical references (p.   ) and index.
   Hardback edition: ISBN-13: 978-1-4222-0196-1
   Paperback edition: ISBN-13: 978-1-4222-0323-1
   1. Who (Musical group)—Juvenile literature. 2. Rock musicians—England—
Juvenile literature. I. Title.
ML3930.W45F59 2008
782.42166092'2—dc22   2007017391

Publisher's notes:
• All quotations in this book come from original sources, and contain the spelling and grammatical inconsistencies of the original text.

• The Web sites mentioned in this book were active at the time of publication. The publisher is not responsible for Web sites that have changed their addresses or discontinued operation since the date of publication. The publisher will review and update the Web site addresses each time the book is reprinted.

CONTENTS

ROCK 'N' ROLL TIMELINE

1951
"Rocket 88," considered by many to be the first rock single, is released by Ike Turner.

1969
The Woodstock Music and Arts Festival attracts a huge crowd to rural upstate New York.

1952
DJ Alan Freed coins and popularizes the term "Rock and Roll," proclaimes himself the "Father of Rock and Roll," and declares, "Rock and Roll is a river of music that has absorbed many streams: rhythm and blues, jazz, rag time, cowboy songs, country songs, folk songs. All have contributed to the Big Beat."

1969
Tommy, the first rock opera, is released by British rock band The Who.

1970
The Beatles break up.

1955
"Rock Around the Clock" by Bill Haley & His Comets is released; it tops the U.S. charts and becomes wildly popular in Britain, Australia, and Germany.

1967
The Monterey Pop Festival in California kicks off open air rock concerts.

1971
Jim Morrison, lead singer of The Doors, dies in Paris.

1965
The psychedelic rock band, the Grateful Dead, is formed in San Francisco.

1971
Duane Allman, lead guitarist of the Allman Brothers Band, dies.

1950s

1960s

1970s

1957
Bill Haley tours Europe.

1969
A rock concert held at Altamont Speedway in California is marred by violence.

1974
Sheer Heart Attack by the British rock band Queen becomes an international success.

1957
Jerry Lee Lewis and Buddy Holly become the first rock musicians to tour Australia.

1969
The Rolling Stones tour America as "The Greatest Rock and Roll Band in the World."

1954
Elvis Presley releases the extremely popular single "That's All Right (Mama)."

1961
The first Grammy for Best Rock 'n' Roll Recording is awarded to Chubby Checker for *Let's Twist Again*.

1974
"Sweet Home Alabama" by Southern rock band Lynyrd Skynyrd is released and becomes an American anthem.

1964
The Beatles make their first visit to America, setting off the British Invasion.

1973
Rolling Stone magazine names Annie Leibovitz chief photographer and "rock 'n' roll photographer;" she follows and photographs rockers Mick Jagger, John Lennon, and others.

1987
Billy Joel becomes the first American rock star to perform in the Soviet Union since the construction of the Berlin Wall.

2005
Led Zeppelin is ranked #1 on VH1's list of the 100 Greatest Artists of Hard Rock.

2005
Many rock groups participate in Live 8, a series of concerts to raise awareness of extreme poverty in Africa.

1985
Rock stars perform at Live Aid, a benefit concert to raise money to fight Ethiopian famine.

2003
Led Zeppelin's "Stairway to Heaven" is inducted into the Grammy Hall of Fame.

1980
John Lennon of the Beatles is murdered in New York City.

2000s
Aerosmith's album sales reach 140 million worldwide and the group becomes the bestselling American hard rock band of all time.

2007
Billy Joel become the first person to sing the National Anthem before two Super Bowls.

1975
Tommy, the movie, is released.

1975
Time magazine features Bruce Springsteen on its cover as "Rock's New Sensation."

1995
The Rock and Roll Hall of Fame and Museum opens in Cleveland, Ohio.

1970s   1980s   1990s   2000s

1979
Pink Floyd's *The Wall* is released.

1991
Freddie Mercury, lead vocalist of the British rock group Queen, dies of AIDS.

2004
Elton John receives a Kennedy Center Honor.

1979
The first Grammy for Best Rock Vocal Performance by a Duo or Group is awarded to The Eagles.

2004
Rolling Stone Magazine ranks The Beatles #1 of the 100 Greatest Artists of All Time, and Bob Dylan #2.

1986
The Rolling Stones receive a Grammy Lifetime Achievement Award.

1981
MTV goes on the air.

2006
U2 wins five more Grammys, for a total of 22—the most of any rock artist or group.

1986
The first Rock and Roll Hall of Fame induction ceremony is held; Chuck Berry, Little Richard, Ray Charles, Elvis Presley, and James Brown, are among the first inductees.

1981
For Those About to Rock We Salute You by Australian rock band AC/DC becomes the first hard rock album to reach #1 in the U.S.

2006
Bob Dylan, at age 65, releases *Modern Times* which immediately rises to #1 in the U.S.

The Who performed in London's Hyde Park for Live 8 on July 2, 2005. The group has a well-earned reputation for playing for worthy causes. The Who has achieved more success than most rock bands ever hope to attain, and its members believe in giving back. Live 8 was another opportunity for them to do so.

The Who Cares

Those in the crowd were getting even more excited as the time neared for the group to take the stage. For many, this was the first time they would see the legendary group. They had been treated to megagroups there in London and through satellite hookups with the other **venues**. Finally, comedian Peter Kay announces, "Here are the Spice Girls!"

Huh?

It was all a gag, an inside commentary about the controversy surrounding the appearance—or nonappearance—of the Spice Girls at this very important event: Live 8. After a correction was given and they were properly introduced, The Who, one of the greatest bands of all time, took the stage. They were there to entertain the massive audience and to help a worthy cause.

Live 8

According to many experts, one of the biggest problems in the world today is the extreme poverty that many of the world's citizens must face every day. This is particularly true in Africa, a continent with many countries plagued by drought and civil unrest.

In May 2005, Bob Geldof, former lead singer of the Irish band Boomtown Rats, announced that a concert would be held on July 2, 2005, the eve of the Group of 8 (G8) summit. The G8 consists of the leaders of the world's most economically successful countries. The purpose of the concert, according to Bob, was to bring attention to the **plight** of those countries that owed the most money to the G8 nations. The goal was to encourage individuals to contact their representatives to the conference and ask them to reduce the debt owed by the poorest nations. Poor countries could not hope to improve other areas of concern—such as lack of food, HIV/AIDS-related issues, and civil conflict—if most of their money went toward repayment of these loans.

The concert was not held to raise funds; rather, its purpose was to raise awareness and to help empower those in the poor nations. According to Bono, frontman for U2 and another **humanitarian activist**:

> **"Live 8 was, and remains a brilliant moment but what is more important is the brilliant movement of which it was a part. This gives the poorest of the poor real political muscle for the first time."**

The concerts held in Philadelphia, London, Rome, Berlin, Paris, and other cities had something for everyone. U2, Madonna, Coldplay, Robbie Williams, George Michael, and Paul McCartney were among those playing for the cause. Even Pink Floyd put away old feuds to re-form and play. The Who was there with an exciting performance of its biggest hits, "Who Are You" and "Won't Get Fooled Again."

The Who and Live Aid

Live 8 was not the first time the group played for causes in which they believed. After many years as a rock legend, The Who had basically disbanded in late 1983. But in July 1985, members came together to perform at the Wembley Stadium venue of another Bob Geldof project, Live Aid. Raising money to help combat the effects of a devastating famine in Ethiopia was the driving force behind this series of concerts. Like Live 8, concerts were held in multiple sites, including Philadelphia, London, and Sydney, Australia. Among the artists performing were the biggest names in music: U2, INXS, Joan Baez, Paul McCartney, Phil Collins, David Bowie, Santana, Mick Jagger, and, of course, The Who.

The crowd at Live 8—both in person and watching on television all over the world—were treated to classic Pete Townshend on guitar. The Who was just one band working to increase awareness of extreme poverty in the world, especially in Africa. For many, poverty caused by drought and civil unrest is a life-and-death battle.

In 1985, Bob Geldof saw images of people starving in Ethiopia, and he didn't like what he saw—men, women, and children who appeared to be dying in front of his eyes. So, he brought together rock's biggest names for Live Aid. Here, at the end of the concert, Pete Townshend and Paul McCartney carry Bob on their shoulders.

Drummer Kenny Jones rejoined the group for the performance at Live Aid. And while the group's set wasn't perfect (many critics claim that "Won't Get Fooled Again" was seriously unrehearsed), fans were thrilled to hear live performances of "My Generation," "Pinball Wizard," Love Reign O'er Me," and even "Won't Get Fooled Again." Well, those who could hear the music enjoyed it. For "My Generation," only those in Wembley Stadium could hear the band; the BBC,

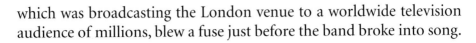

which was broadcasting the London venue to a worldwide television audience of millions, blew a fuse just before the band broke into song.

The Who and New York

On September 11, 2001, life changed for countless people in many countries when terrorists attacked the World Trade Center in New York City and the Pentagon outside Washington, D.C. A third plane crashed in the Pennsylvania countryside before it could reach its target.

In the aftermath of the attacks, many concerts and other events were held to raise funds and encourage the spirits of those affected by the attacks. In October of 2001, many gathered at New York City's Madison Square Garden for the Concert for New York City. Most in the audience were New York City firefighters or police officers, or family members of those who were lost or injured while trying to save others. Also honored that evening were the rescue workers who were still doing everything they could to recover bodies for the families of those lost in the tragedy.

Organized by Paul McCartney, those performing that evening were among the who's who of the music world. Destiny's Child, Billy Joel, Melissa Etheridge, Elton John, Eric Clapton, Bon Jovi, Jay-Z, and the Goo Goo Dolls were among the musicians who honored those assembled and those who could not be there. The Who sang "Who Are You," and the audience went wild. According to most critics and reviewers, The Who's performance was the audience's most enthusiastically received of the evening, by far.

The Who has been around for more than forty years, and they are still incredibly popular. That's an incredible accomplishment for a group that started as a detour.

If you loved music and playing an instrument, the 1960s were a great time. It seemed as though every young person in Great Britain (and the United States, too) wanted to be a rock star. Among the budding legends were (left to right) Pete Townshend, Roger Daltrey, Keith Moon, and John Entwistle. They would succeed; many others would not.

2

Early Who

The sixties were a great time for music. It was also a decade of rapid change. What was popular one week sometimes seemed to have been eclipsed by another style the next. Band membership and names changed so often you needed a scorecard to keep track. These were exciting years for those in the music industry.

Among those in England working toward a career in music were Roger Daltrey, Pete Townshend, John Entwistle, and Keith Moon. Roger had the potential to be excellent at his schoolwork, but he had problems with authority figures. Once he discovered the guitar and rock music, any hopes his parents had that Roger would go to college were dashed. In fact, he was kicked out of school when his preoccupation with music meant he could no longer concentrate on his studies. Meanwhile, Pete came from a musical family; his father played sax with the Squadronaires, and his mother was a singer. Pete became enthralled with American rock from an early age. John had also been exposed to music from an early age and had learned to play the trumpet, french horn, and piano while he was still quite young. Keith, however, had difficulty with hyperactivity while a child, and nothing seemed to be able to hold his attention. One of his teachers didn't hold out much hope for Keith's ability, calling him "Retarded artistically. Idiotic in other respects." But Keith's musical ability brought him praise. On one report card, a teacher noted, "he has great ability, but must guard against a tendency to show off." Keith didn't graduate.

Becoming The Who—But First . . .

In the late 1950s, Roger formed his first group, the Detours. Once he was asked to leave school, Roger had to get a job to support his music habit, and he became a sheet-metal worker. Most days, he'd leave his day job and go practice with the group in the evening. After a while, the Detours became popular rock/skiffle band at weddings and bars. (Skiffle music, a very popular style of music in Britain during the 1950s and 1960s, was a form of folk music that added bits of jazz and blues to its sound.)

In 1961, Pete and John, who had known each other since grammar school, formed their first band, the Confederates. Pete played the banjo, and John played horn instruments. The duo played Dixieland music, a form of jazz that developed in the American South. Pete and John went on to play together with the Aristocrats and the Scorpions. But, fame wouldn't find them—or Roger—until they all met.

By 1964, Roger had met John. He was impressed with John's musical skills and asked him to join the Detours. John saw it as a great opportunity and agreed. But he wanted Pete to join as well. With John and Pete on board, the group consisted of Roger on lead guitar, Pete on rhythm guitar, John on bass, Doug Sandom on drums, and Colin Dawson singing leads. But, when Colin left the group, Roger moved over to provide the vocals for the group, and Pete became the lead guitarist.

The band members weren't happy with the name Detours, so, like many other groups, they decided to change it. Pete's roommate suggested The Who, and everyone agreed. From then on, except for

In the 1950s and 1960s, bands changed names and members more often than some people change socks. The Who didn't escape that trend. The seeds of the group that would become a rock legend were planted with the Detours, from left, Pete Townshend, John Entwistle, Colin Dawson, Doug Sandom, and Roger Daltrey.

a very brief period when they changed it to the High Notes (and quickly back again), the group has been called The Who.

The year 1964 brought another change to the group, this one in personnel. David decided to leave the group, and the remaining members found themselves in search of a drummer. For a while, they used a session drummer to fill in for the gigs they already had scheduled. During one of those shows, seventeen-year-old Keith Moon was in the audience. Once they saw him audition, there was no question that he should join the group; he played so energetically, he practically smashed the drum set to smithereens! Keith had been playing in groups since he was twelve, but his most recent gig had been with the Beachcombers, a group that performed **covers** of songs done by Cliff Richards. Now, with a lineup of Pete, Roger, John, and Keith, The Who was set, and would be so for the next fourteen years.

THE WHO

When Keith Moon joined the group as drummer, both the band's name and membership were set for the next few years. Now the guys could concentrate on making music, and that they did. Roger, Pete, John, and Keith began the journey that would make them rock superstars and an important part of rock history.

And the Leader Is . . .

Roger Daltrey may be small of build, but he is not one to be treated lightly. He had his ideas, and he expected things to be done his way. In Geoffrey Giuliano's book *Behind Blue Eyes: The Life of Pete Townshend*, Pete is quoted as saying that Roger "ran things the way he wanted. If you argued with him, you usually got a bunch of fives." And Roger wasn't afraid to punch those who disagreed with him!

Roger wasn't the only one, though, with ideas about how things should be with the band. Pete's talent as a songwriter quickly surfaced, and most of the other band members looked at him as the group's main songwriter. That would have been fine, but Roger wasn't always happy with what Pete turned out. Roger, as group leader (even if self-proclaimed only), took it upon himself to select most of the songs the band performed. He often chose Beatles' tunes; after all, it was impossible to argue with the success they were having with the songs. But Roger also liked Motown artists such as James Brown.

When Pete wrote a song, he tried to **infuse** it with meaning, depth. His songs also tended to challenge the ability of the band. He didn't want the group to become lazy, playing the same type of music over and over again. For the most part, John and Keith tried to stay out of the controversy, though Keith was a big fan of California surf music.

There could be no denying that tensions often ran high between Roger and Pete; at times, Roger would be so upset about one of Pete's compositions that he'd simply refuse to sing it, leaving it to Pete to do so.

The Mods

In 1964, The Who released a single called "Zoot Suit/I'm the Face" under the name the High Numbers. The song was aimed toward the Mods, who had quickly become fans of the band. Though the single crashed and burned, failing to make the charts (and prompting the group to retake the name The Who), it helped establish the group as *the* band preferred by members of the British Mods.

The Mod **subculture** began in London during the late 1950s. Originally, the term described individuals who liked modern jazz. Later, the definition grew to include elements of music, art, and even fashion. The trend began among middle-class teenagers who had family connections within the garment and fashion industries. Though some girls were involved, most were boys in the early days of Mod. These boys appreciated high-quality fashion, especially suits that were designed and made in Italy.

Clubs such as London's The Scene and The Flamingo were the hotbeds of Mods activity. Young people would gather at the all-night clubs, party, show off their clothes, and practice the latest dance moves. Their energetic lifestyle sometimes required a little extra boost

Besides being a great time for musicians, the sixties were also a time of cultural change. In London, the Mods loved to party at the most popular clubs, show off their clothes, dance, and at time, indulge in some drug use. The Mods' band of choice was The Who, seen in this photo dancing with some of its Mods fans.

in the form of **amphetamines**. The Mods often traveled between clubs on scooters, some sprouting many mirrors.

Before long, the Mod lifestyle grew beyond the middle class to encompass all economic and social classes. Soul, ska, and bluebeat styles of music joined the scene, and sometimes replaced the jazz and rhythm and blues that had been the favorites of many early Mods. These young adults championed a British form of rhythm and blues, the music that groups like The Who, Small Faces, the Kinks, and the Yardbirds performed. The Who often smashed their equipment after a performance, something the Mods also enjoyed.

By the summer of 1966, things had changed both in London and the world. The things the Mods stood for didn't seem quite as important,

Members of The Who were quite impressed when Keith almost smashed his drums to bits at the audition. Before long, other members of the band began bashing their instruments after performances. In this photo, Pete is shown ready to bash his guitar. Eventually, other groups followed The Who's lead, and many musical instruments were sacrificed in the name of entertainment.

and the culture had begun to take on a more leisurely, laid-back approach to life. The groups that had been identified with the movement changed as well, and the Mods who had been an integral force just two years before began to evolve into something and someone else.

Finding a Hit

In 1965, The Who released the single "I Can't Explain," which became the group's first hit. The group followed that single with "Anyway, Anyhow, Anywhere" and "Substitute." The songs touched teenagers around the world, giving them something to which they could relate. According to the Rock and Roll Hall of Fame:

> **"The early Who demonstrated a mastery of the three-minute single, articulating the frustrations of adolescence."**

The key was the "three-minute single." To make a connection with the kids, the recordings needed to be played on the radio. Most radio stations were unwilling to play anything longer than three minutes. The Who had successfully found the way to get on the radio.

The Who's first big-selling album was *The Who Sings My Generation*, released in the United States in 1965. Again, the songs connected with those who purchased the albums—teens. The album was also a hit with reviewers. According to *Rolling Stone*:

> **"*The Who Sings My Generation* became the blueprint for much of the subsequent garage rock, heavy metal, and punk. In contrast to the debut albums of the Stones (whose take on Southern American rock & soul was fairly earnest) and Beatles (who spread the word of rock & roll through sweet harmonies and easily digestible melodies), *My Generation* positively shoved at the boundaries of popular music. Townshend's fiercely original guitar experiments here predate the innovations of his later American rival Jimi Hendrix."**

In the mid-1960s, the songs covered more edgy topics, thanks to Pete's songwriting abilities. "I'm a Boy" was about a boy dressed up like a girl, and "Pictures of Lily" was about masturbation. The group's song "Happy Jack." cracked the U.S. top-40 charts in 1967.

Getting Longer

As the 1960s neared its end, The Who closed out one facet of their music and set out to establish another trend—under Pete's direction. His songs had become increasingly controversial. He began to work on longer songs, songs that some radio stations might hesitate to play because of their length. Pete began thinking of the albums as a book, with each track acting as a chapter. Like most books, though the chapters might stand alone, one could not understand the true,

Ah, the life of a rock star. All right, it can mean lots of hard work and long hours, but you have to admit that it has its perks. In this photo from 1968, the guys are shown posing on a London train with some attractive models. But, they *are* working; it's a promotional shoot for a new album.

The Who made rock music history in 1969 when *Tommy* became the first commercially and critically successful rock opera in history. The story of a deaf, dumb, and blind boy, *Tommy* was the fulfillment of one of Pete's dreams. In this photograph, Roger sings his heart out during a performance of the rock opera.

complex intention of the author/composer without listening to them in context with each other. Though this was something many other groups dared not do, The Who found success in the longer format. *A Quick One* and *The Who Sell Out* each contained mini-rock operas. *The Who Sell Out* even had jingles and commercials, as though it was being played on the radio. That album also brought The Who its biggest hit in the United States: "I Can See for Miles."

Tommy and Rock Festivals

The Who's fame in America grew quickly. They appeared at the Monterey Pop Festival in 1967, and fans got to see the group perform— and destroy their equipment—in person. Television viewers got to see similar destruction as well as an exploding drum set when the group performed on *The Smothers Brothers Comedy Hour*, also in 1967.

But the group was about more than destroying guitars and drums, and Pete had a dream. When Pete was interviewed by *Rolling Stone*, in the magazine's first interview, he told the reporter he was working on something special, a full-length rock opera. Pete's dream came true in 1969 with *Tommy*, the first commercially and critically successful rock opera. Inspired by spiritual teachings of Meher Baba, Pete sat down and wrote the phenomenal piece of music. According to *Life* magazine:

> **"for sheer power, invention and brilliance of performance, *Tommy* outstrips anything which has ever come out of a recording studio."**

The album reached #4 on the charts in the United States.

The Who played most of the opera at the Woodstock Music and Art Festival in 1969. The concert was held in Max Yasgur's field and attracted an estimated 500,000 people from all over the country. For four days, concertgoers listened to music, danced, got high, and got drunk while listening to some of the biggest names in rock. The Who joined artists such as Jimi Hendrix, the Jefferson Airplane, and Joe Cocker at the concert.

The Who's Woodstock performance from *Tommy* was memorable. When the film of the concert was released, more people were able to learn about the mysterious "deaf, dumb and blind boy [who] sure plays a mean pinball."

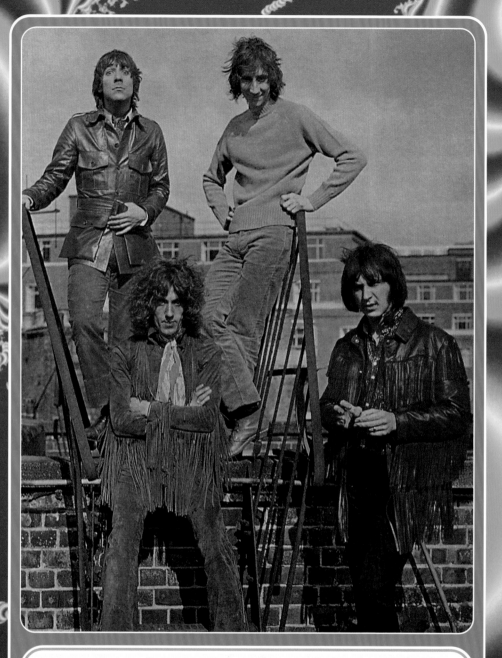

If The Who was hot in the 1960s, it was scorching hot in the 1970s. While some groups struggled, others—like The Who—seemed to have their fingers on the pulse of the music-loving and -buying public. But that didn't mean the group didn't have problems. The band had its own battles to fight.

3

Who's Unique

The 1960s had been good for The Who. Roger, Pete, Keith, and John might have not seen eye to eye on everything, and they had their own tastes in music, but there was no question that together, they were formidable. And the 1960s was just a hint of the success The Who would find during the next decade.

Live at Leeds

Tommy remained strong in 1970, giving the group a #12 charting with "See Me, Feel Me." But Roger, Pete, Keith, and John weren't content basking in the success of *Tommy*. After all, not all the critics had been particularly kind. A reviewer for *Rolling Stone* wrote:

> **"*Tommy* isn't the masterpiece it was hyped to be when it first appeared. There's no doubting its excellence as a narrative-based set of Who songs, but it's not nearly as much fun, or even as enlightening, as *Sell Out*."**

So the group moved on. The group's performances at Monterey, Woodstock, and other concerts had solidified its reputation as a live band. To take advantage of the attention they had received for their live performances, The Who put together a live album, *Live at Leeds*. *Rolling Stone* called the album, cleverly packaged to look like a **bootleg**, "a brutal . . . performance set." Many critics have called the album the best live rock album of all time.

Lighthouse

The band began work on a new studio album during the summer of 1970. They had laid down about half the tracks before Pete's attention was directed to another project, an album and performance art project. Pete had attended art school, and his interest in the visual arts had not lessened though his career had taken another direction. After writing the song "Pure and Easy" for the project, Pete's attention was completely taken away from the studio album.

Despite Pete's intentions, the Lighthouse project never materialized in the way he had wanted. In 1971, The Who did record some of the Lighthouse material and a song by John for the album *Who's Next*. The group also released other songs Pete had written for the project as singles on albums by The Who and on Pete's solo albums. And though Pete's original plan for the project did not come about, the BBC did broadcast a version of the Lighthouse production in 2000. Fans could order a six-CD set of the production from Pete's Web site.

Who's Next

Many groups' albums are either well-received by the public or well-reviewed by the critics, but not both. There was no such problem with The Who's album *Who's Next*, which reached #4 on the U.S. album charts. According to some reviewers, *Who's Next* was the release that set The Who apart from other groups that were part of the British Invasion. According to *Rolling Stone*:

According to *Rolling Stone, Who's Next* made The Who "arena rock gods." The album set the band apart from all of the other groups coming out of Britain in the early 1970s. Fans who came to a Who concert were treated to a performance they could not find anywhere else.

"The Who was at a turning point in 1971, straddling the transition from British Invasion pioneers to arena-rock gods. On *Who's Next*, the band crossed that line with power and grace."

The Rock and Roll Hall of Fame calls the album

"a flawless album of discreet numbers that helped define the sound and sensibility of rock in the Seventies. From 'Baba O'Riley's album-opening synth-propelled discourse on 'teenage wasteland' through to Daltrey's electrifying scream on the closing track, 'Won't Get Fooled Again,' *Who's Next* stands as a virtual rock **primer**."

Before *Who's Next*, according to these critics, The Who was just another British group that had found tremendous success with audiences in the United States during the 1960s. But the album put them in another category.

The Beatles and the Rolling Stones had started the British Invasion, and it soon grew to the point that American bands were virtually ignored by music lovers and critics in their own country. But one of the criticisms that grew as the British Invasion took hold in the United States was that the groups tended to sound alike. After *Who's Next*, that was not a criticism that could be directed toward The Who.

Many groups had been using a synthesizer to manipulate their sound. *Who's Next* was one of the first successful albums, however, that used the synthesizer as an instrument itself, in the same way musicians used drums, guitars, the bass, and keyboards. Pete's compositions moved the synthesizer from special-effects machine to music-making instrument, and fans and critics both liked the result. The album's "Won't Get Fooled Again" became the first hit single in which the synthesizer played a dominate part.

Back to Rock Opera

The Who followed up *Who's Next* with a return to rock opera—in a way. *Quadrophenia*, which was released in 1973, has been described as

Tommy had been a big success for The Who, and the group decided to try another one. *Quadrophenia* was the story of a boy with multiple personalities, told within the context of a real-life incident. The critics didn't care for it, but they had to admit that only The Who could even come close to pulling it off.

a monologue because most of the spoken parts are by one character, rather than several, as would be expected in an opera.

   Quadrophenia tells the story of one boy, Jimmy, who is struggling to find his identity while dealing with multiple personality disorder; he has four distinct personalities. Jimmy's story is told amid the conflict between the Mods and the Rockers, a real-life incident in British history of the 1960s.

   Critics liked *Quadrophenia* less than *Tommy*. Some felt the story was weak. But while they might not have liked the album, they recognized that no other group could have come close to pulling off such a production. And some of the songs, including "The Real Me," "The Punk and the Godfather," and "Love, Reign O'er Me," were undeniably good.

The Soul of Pete Townshend

Though Roger Daltrey was for many the face of The Who, and he was the group's leader and frontman, the songs were coming primarily from Pete. Pete's songs often described the **angst** of being an outsider, of having trouble fitting in with the world.

Spirituality also played a role in Pete's songs. In the late 1960s, Pete had become aware of an Indian guru named Meher Baba. As a child, Baba had shown no inclination toward becoming a spiritual leader; he was like most young people living in his circumstances at his time. But, according to the Baba story, one day when the nineteen-year-old was riding his bicycle, he was kissed on the forehead by a very old Muslim woman who was a spiritual master. That kiss opened Baba to his own spirituality.

Baba mixed elements of Vedantic and Sufi **mysticism** in his teachings. He taught that no matter how much one studied God intellectually, the only way to truly know God was through love. He is perhaps best known for his hard stance against drug use, especially the use of LSD, which was seriously increasing during the late 1960s and 1970s. This teaching was harder for Pete to follow, as he had a history of drug use.

From 1925 until 1969, Baba did not speak at all. At first, he used an alphabet board to communicate. Eventually, however, he gave up the board and used a set of hand signals to "speak" with others. Despite his choice to forgo traditional methods of communication, Baba traveled extensively to spread his message.

Baba is listed as Avatar, a coauthor of *Tommy*. Pete also wrote the song "Baba O'Riley," which appears on *Who's Next*, for the spiritual leader. Those familiar with Baba's teachings and Pete's interest in them searched other songs for the guru's influence.

Tommy on Film

In 1975, fans were treated to *The Who by Numbers*. Though some reviewers considered the album to be a safe one by the group—a rehashing of tried and true ideas—"Squeeze Box" was a breakout hit single. The biggest event for the group that year was the debut of its rock opera *Tommy* as a film directed by the legendary Ken Russell.

Roger starred in the movie as Tommy. Movie veterans Oliver Reed, Ann-Margaret, and Jack Nicholson also starred. And the film

It was only a matter of time before *Tommy* the movie was made. Some of the biggest rock stars of the time—including members of The Who—performed in the film. The film won Academy Award nominations for lead actress and score. Ann-Margaret won a Golden Globe for her performance. Roger was also nominated for a Globe.

featured numerous recording artists as well: Eric Clapton played the Preacher, Elton John was the Local Lad, and Tina Turner appeared as the Acid Queen. Keith played Uncle Ernie, and Pete and John played themselves in the film.

Fans loved the movie! So did the Academy of Motion Picture Arts and Sciences—the Oscars®. Ann-Margaret was nominated for Best Actress in a Leading Role, and Pete received a nomination for Best Music, Scoring Original Song Score and/or Adaptation. Though the film didn't win any Oscars, it had better luck with the Hollywood Foreign Press Association. Ann-Margaret won the group's Golden Globe® in the Best Motion Picture Actress-Musical/Comedy category. Roger was nominated for Best Motion Picture Debut in a Motion Picture-Male, and the film received a nomination for Best Motion Picture-Musical/Comedy.

Who Are You wasn't a huge hit with critics, and some thought it was time for the guys to call it quits. They'd had a good run, but perhaps it was time for something new and fresh. Obviously, the critics were a bit premature, though the group's sound would change after Keith died.

Losing the Moon

It seemed as though The Who was riding high on the success of the film and the sales of *The Who by Numbers*. Crowds still flocked to the group's concerts, and in 1976, a concert at Charlton Athletic Football Ground was certified by the folks at the *Guinness Book of World Records* as the loudest concert. It held that distinction for more than ten years.

Despite the continuing success of the group, some critics were beginning to wonder if The Who was losing its edge musically. *Rolling Stone* said the group was

"delivering slick, high-quality album-oriented rock and singer/songwriter fare but no longer pushing boundaries."

The group's next album, *Who Are You*, contained songs that were more likely to receive radio airplay, since they were shorter. Rather than relieving qualms that the group was on its downslide, *Rolling Stone* called it and its predecessor "decent," with

"mixes of great, good, and mediocre material. But Townshend's heart no longer seemed to be in the songwriting, and Daltrey's commanding voice had become a parody of itself."

Continuing its success wasn't the group's only concern. Keith had a serious problem with destructive behavior. He had a reputation for destroying hotel rooms and even his own houses. According to some reports, he even enjoyed throwing explosives down a toilet and watching them blow up. Sometimes Keith was under the influence of drugs or alcohol, but at other times it appears as though it was just Keith being Keith.

There was no question that Keith had problems with alcohol. His death on September 7, 1978, was the result of his trying to solve that problem. Keith and his girlfriend had attended the preview of *The Buddy Holly Story* with Paul and Linda McCartney, followed by dinner. After Keith returned home, he apparently took an over-dose of Clomethiazole, a drug he was taking to help him kick his addiction to alcohol. Keith Moon was thirty-two years old.

After Keith

The band needed to replace Keith, and the group chose Kenney Jones, formerly with the groups Small Faces and Faces, to play the drums. The group continued to tour, and concerts in London and New York City were great successes. A Cincinnati concert in December 1979, however, was not such a success. In a crush for

In 1979, *The Kids Are Alright* opened at the prestigious Cannes Film Festival. The film gives an inside look at the birth and growth of The Who. It features the last recorded performance by Keith Moon, as well as cameos by comedian Tommy Smothers and musicians Keith Richards and Ringo Starr.

seats, eleven fans were killed. No one told the band about the tragedy until after the concert. The deaths deeply affected each of the guys.

That same December, the group became the third band to appear on the cover of *Time* magazine. Another Who album found its way to film in 1979 when *Quadrophenia* was released. It was a commercial success and has become a cult classic for Who and Keith Moon fans.

Still a Place for The Who?

As the 1980s began, things began to change in the music world, and The Who tried to adapt their sound to accommodate the change. The more pop-oriented albums received some critical praise, but fans didn't like the new sound. They were still attached to the type of music that had made The Who great—and unique.

In 1982, Pete, Stevie Nicks, Mick Jagger, Adam Ant, Pat Benatar, the Police, and David Bowie kicked off the "I Want My MTV" campaign. Concerts wouldn't be as important to a group's success; they had been replaced with slick videos. The Who had always been a phenomenal live band, and doubt grew about the group's ability to continue.

Pete had a life change in 1982 as well. He admitted that he was an alcoholic. He got sober, and the group went on a large tour. After the tour, Pete wanted to turn The Who into a studio-only group, one that existed only to record.

The tour was a success, and Pete began 1983 writing songs for The Who's next album. But things didn't go well; Pete just couldn't do it. He felt nothing he wrote was good enough for The Who. In December, he issued a statement: he was leaving the group.

Campaign '82's Biggest Lies   **'Eating Raoul'**

Rolling Stone

ISSUE NO. 382
NOVEMBER 11TH, 1982
$1.50 U.S. 90¢

THE WHO
THE END

As The Who entered the 1980s, Kenney Jones played drums for the group. In 1982, the new Who appeared on the cover of *Rolling Stone*: left to right, Kenney, Roger, Pete, and John. Not long after the magazine appeared, however, The Who retired. But it wouldn't be the end of the group.

Who Re-Formed

The result of Pete's announcement was simple: without Pete Townshend, there would be no Who. Though others had contributed songs the group had performed, Pete had written the ones that had been most successful. And now, without Pete, what would they be? It didn't seem possible the group could go on.

So it didn't. The band that had been such an innovator in rock music retired. But that didn't mean its members did.

Pete

Pete had ventured into solo and group projects while he had been with The Who. Along with other followers of Baba, Pete had recorded three albums about his teachings: *Happy Birthday*, *I Am*, and *With Love*. The albums were recorded between 1969 and 1971.

In 1972, Pete released his first major-label solo album, *Who Came First.* The album featured Who **demos** and highlighted Pete as an **acoustic** guitarist. The album wasn't a huge success, but it had respectable sales.

In 1980, Pete Townshend, solo artist, had his biggest hit to date with the album *Empty Glass.* "Let My Love Open the Door" made it to the top-10 single list. *All the Best Cowboys Have Chinese Eyes* followed with its hit "Slit Skirts." Pete hadn't given up on the rock opera, either. In 1985, he released *White City: A Novel*, which included performances by John and Roger.

But Pete didn't just write and perform music during this interlude away from The Who. Pete Townshend, author, also appeared. In 1984, Pete published a collection of short stories called *Horse's Neck.* This wouldn't be his last book either.

Roger

Like Pete, Roger had ventured into solo projects while with The Who. In 1973, *Daltrey* spun-off Roger's first solo hit single, "Giving It All Away." The song reached #5 in the UK; *Daltrey* cracked the U.S. album charts at #50.

Daltrey was followed with more albums that made it to the U.S. album charts. His highest charting solo album was 1980's *McVicar*, which reached #22. The album was a soundtrack for a film he produced and in which he starred. Pete, John, and Kenney also appeared on the album. In 1985, Roger released an album in honor of Keith, *Under a Raging Moon*, which charted at #42 in the United States.

But also like Pete, Roger used the time apart from The Who to expand into another area. For Roger, that was acting. *Tommy* was not Roger's first experience as an actor. In 1975, he had appeared as the composer Franz Liszt in *Lisztomania.* During the years away from The Who, Roger appeared in the films *The Legacy, McVicar, The Beggar's Opera*, and *Murder: Ultimate Grounds for Divorce*, as well as on several television programs. And holding true to his desire to be the leader, Roger also ventured into producing.

John

John was one of the most **prolific** when it came to solo music projects. Before the band retired, he had already released five solo albums. All

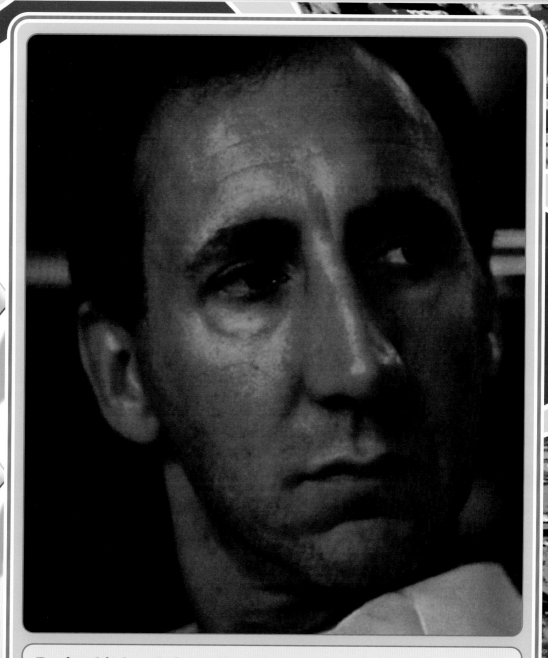

During his break from The Who, Pete kept busy. He recorded solo albums, worked as a book editor, and wrote a collection of short stories and a book of poetry. He wrote and recorded a rock opera, *White City: A Novel*. The album reflected his belief that an album should be considered a book, with the individual tracks its chapters.

A KEN RUSSELL FILM STARRING ROGER DALTREY

LISZTOMANIA

Perhaps one of the busiest Who members during the group's break was Roger Daltrey. Though he recorded solo projects, Roger spent a lot of time acting. His first try at acting was as Hungarian composer Franz Liszt in *Lisztomania* in 1975. Now, with time away from The Who, Roger appeared in several films and on British television.

of them charted in the United States, but none hit higher than #71. He also recorded with other top-name artists, such as Alice Cooper.

But John's talents weren't limited to music. He had been an art student, and during his time away from The Who, he worked on developing his skills as a graphic artist.

Together Again

Many of the people of Ethiopia were starving, and it seemed as though few people were actually paying attention. But some were, and more important, they weren't about to sit back and let someone else do something about the problem.

One of those who were listening was Bob Geldof. He called on the biggest names in music to perform at a multi-venue concert called Live Aid. One of the bands that was quick to say yes was The Who.

The group hadn't formally played together since 1983, but the guys had stayed in touch, even playing on each other's recordings. But the July 13, 1985 performance would be the first time since 1983 that they performed as The Who. Though the live crowd was thrilled with the performance, it wasn't enough for the guys to commit to re-forming. That would take another few years.

Together Again—For Real (Kind Of)

The guys had gone back to their various solo projects after Live Aid. Then, in 1988, the British Phonography Industry honored the group with its Lifetime Achievement Award. The band played a few numbers at the ceremony, and the seeds were sown for a reunion.

In 1989, The Who embarked on a reunion tour. Kenney Jones was replaced on drums by Simon Phillips, who had worked with Pete for many years. The response to the group's decision to tour was more than anyone could have anticipated.

With more than two million tickets sold, the tour was an unqualified success. Venues all over the country were filled to capacity with fans eager to see the group perform highlights from *Tommy*. The Who played a four-night sell-out stand at Giant Stadium in New York. *Newsweek* magazine stated: "The Who tour is special because, after the Beatles and the Stones, they're IT."

And obviously the fans could not have agreed more.

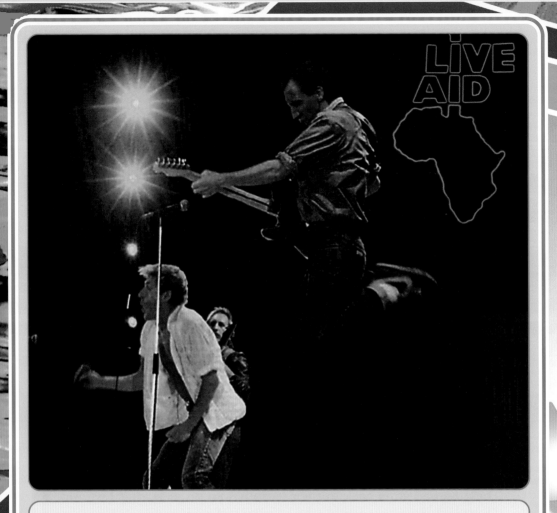

For the first time in two years, The Who came together again to play for a worthy cause: 1985's Live Aid. The benefit concerts raised a great deal of money for—and awareness of—the devastating famine in Ethiopia. Although Who fans were enthusiastic and loud, any hopes for a reunion did not materialize.

The Hall of Fame

In sports as well as in many forms of music and other arts, the ultimate sign of success is election to a hall of fame. For rock musicians, it's inclusion in the Rock and Roll Hall of Fame, located in Cleveland, Ohio.

Like those who become members of the Baseball Hall of Fame, the Football Hall of Fame, and similar halls, membership in the Rock and Roll Hall of Fame has to be earned. Inductees have to meet the tough standards the nominating committee of the Rock and Roll Hall of Fame requires just to put a musician's name on the ballot. According to Rock and Roll Hall of Fame rules, twenty-five years must have passed since a potential nominee's first recording. Those considered for nomination must have made a significant contribution to the development of rock music. Those who meet the criteria are placed on the ballot, which is sent to music experts all over the world. To be inducted, the nominee must have the most votes, and be selected on more than 50 percent of the ballots.

For some, it takes many tries to make it into the Rock and Roll Hall of Fame, if they ever do. For other musicians, such as The Who, their contributions are so great—and so obvious—that they make it into the hall in their first year of eligibility. According to the Rock and Roll Hall of Fame:

> **❝The Who reigned across the decades as one of the greatest rock and roll bands of all time. At their best, they distilled the pent-up energy and chaos of rock and roll into its purest form while investing their music with literary wiles and visionary insight. In their prime they were a unit whose individual personalities fused into a larger-than-life whole.❞**

The Who entered the hall in 1990, along with other music heavy-weights Hank Ballard, Bobby Darin, the Four Seasons, the Four Tops, the Kinks, the Platters, and Simon and Garfunkel. Adam Clayton of the Irish group U2 presented The Who at the Rock and Roll Hall of Fame induction ceremony at the Waldorf Astoria Hotel in New York City.

The following year, The Who covered "Saturday Night's Alright for Fighting" by Elton John for a tribute album, but that was the last time they got together for the next five years.

Together Again—For Real (Maybe)

Once again, the guys went off to do their own things, though there were hints that perhaps the latest retirement would not be the last. When Pete toured in 1993 to promote his latest solo album, for example, John showed up to perform on some of the songs. When the group's thirtieth anniversary came around in 1994, it seemed natural that the guys would regroup for an anniversary tour. Didn't happen. But in celebration of Roger's fiftieth birthday, John and Pete showed up to perform at his two-date Carnegie Hall concerts, though the three didn't perform together as a group. In late 1994, Roger began the Daltrey Sings Townshend tour, with John as a special guest. There were discussions that Roger and John would perform as The Who, and though Pete told Roger that was all right with him, Roger decided against doing so.

Two years later, a former Who hit brought the group together again. Pete was scheduled to perform at a major concert in London's Hyde Park. His initial inclination was to perform an acoustic version of *Quadrophenia*. But then he found out how many people were expected to come to the concert—150,000. He decided his solo performance wouldn't work, so he called Roger and John, who agreed to perform—this one time. Pete's brother Simon played guitar, Zak Starkey (the son of Ringo Starr) played drums, and John "Rabbit" Bundrick was on keyboards. Other musicians came on board so that a "real" production of the rock opera could take place. The performance was a gigantic hit.

There was no arguing with success, and the guys reworked the show and took it on tour in the United States and Europe. After the tour, the group parted again, with the guys going their separate ways. Roger went on tour performing songs by The Who with the British Rock Symphony. John toured with his group, the John Entwistle Band, and Pete performed in shows that highlighted his acoustic skills.

Together Again—For Real (Really)

No matter what they did on their own—or how successful those efforts were—it seemed as though there was no way the guys could stay apart. In 1999, The Who came together again. Roger, Pete, and John were joined by Zak and Rabbit for a series of small concerts to benefit charities. Audiences were treated to The Who classics, including songs that some in the audience were too young to remember!

Even when there was no Who, Roger, John, and Pete (left to right, on the cover of *The Hits Are Alright* from 1997) could not stay apart. They even performed on each other's solo projects. In 1999, they made it official, and The Who re-formed, for good. Zak Starkey, son of Who friend Ringo Starr, was on the drums.

This time it really was inevitable. The band had to get together again, and in 2000, The Who toured the United States and the United Kingdom to huge crowds and nothing but rave reviews. Though Pete, John, and Roger had aged, their music had withstood the test of time.

In 2001, The Who performed at The Concert for New York City and received a Lifetime Achievement Award from the Grammys. The band members talked about a new album, and a tour was set for the following summer.

Tragedy Strikes

The band was eager to begin its summer tour in 2002. But things were not going to go as planned. Just one day before the tour was to begin, John Entwistle was found dead in his Las Vegas hotel room. According to the coroner, John died from a heart attack. Though that was the official cause of death, most believe that the heart attack itself was caused by some bad habits John had. Like many of his generation, John had a long history of cocaine use. He also had high blood pressure and had been a heavy smoker for most of his life.

The band decided to postpone the tour for a while, but they knew they had to go on. And they did, with Pino Palladino playing bass. The tour was a huge success—as usual. In September, Q magazine declared that The Who was one of the "50 Bands to See Before You Die."

Moving On

The Who had always been a major draw on the tour circuit, and in 2004 they toured again. When the group headlined the Isle of Wight Festival, it received rave reviews, something the band was learning to expect.

But things didn't always run completely smoothly for the group. In 2003, Pete came to the attention of British police for some Internet activity. According to statements, Pete was being investigated for child pornography. Pete explained in statements and on his Web site that he was researching a book speaking out *against* child pornography. He wasn't charged. Though the anti-pornography book project has been abandoned, Pete is working on his autobiography. Excerpts are available on his blog, www.petetownshend-whohe.blogspot.com.

Tragedy struck The Who again in 2002, when John Entwistle died just before a tour. But The Who knew what John would want—the tour to continue—and Roger and Pete carried on. The group has performed almost nonstop since its re-formation.

With Pete's problem behind them, The Who announced that they would record an album—their first in more than twenty years—in 2005. The album, *Endless Wire*, was delayed until 2006. In October 2006, The Who was the recipient of the first annual Freddie Mercury Lifetime Achievement in Live Music Award. The award is named after the Queen frontman, who died in 1991. In keeping with the spirit of the award, and to support the new album, The Who toured during 2006 and 2007. A few concerts had to be canceled because Roger became ill, but the tour received rave reviews—of course.

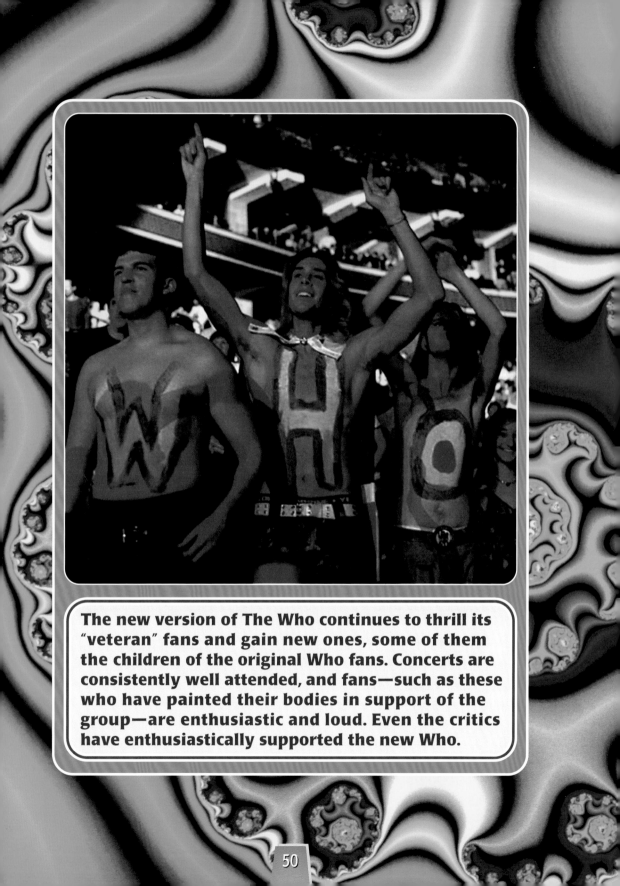

The new version of The Who continues to thrill its "veteran" fans and gain new ones, some of them the children of the original Who fans. Concerts are consistently well attended, and fans—such as these who have painted their bodies in support of the group—are enthusiastic and loud. Even the critics have enthusiastically supported the new Who.

Who Influences Whom?

"Imitation is the sincerest form of flattery." How many times have you heard that about someone or something? If the cliché is true—and a bit of truth is what makes a cliché a cliché—then The Who and its music must be one of the most flattered rock groups ever!

When The Who first became famous, one of the things that made Pete, Keith, John, and Roger unique was their musical aggressiveness. They weren't afraid to take chances, do something different . . . even destroy their equipment! Other bands, like Cream, Led Zeppelin, and Rush took their lead from these pioneers.

The Who and Punk

The Who also influenced most of the punk bands that achieved success. Punk, a music genre popular in the 1970s, featured fast music played very loudly. Lyrics were often "in your face"; punk musicians were not afraid to sing what they believed, and to do it "rudely." The Who's early work is often cited by music historians as the beginning of what would eventually evolve into punk.

Three bands are considered to have been the best of the punk movement. Each of them, the Clash, the Ramones, and the Sex Pistols, were all influenced by The Who. According to historians, The Who is the only influence those groups share. More recently, Green Day has cited The Who as a major influence on its music.

The Rock Opera

The Who was the first group to have a successful rock opera. Whether that was a good thing is debatable. According to *Rolling Stone*,

> **"*Tommy*'s biggest crime is that it inspired lesser artists to attempt the same trick, and by the late '70s, bands like Styx had turned operatic concept albums into rock's lamest joke."**

Whether lame or inspiring, The Who's rock operas led groups like David Bowie, Pink Floyd, and more recently Green Day, to record their own forms of the genre.

Other Influences

The influence of The Who went beyond punk bands and rock operas. U2's Bono claims, "More than any other band, The Who are our role models." Pearl Jam's Eddie Vedder states:

> **"The one thing that disgusts me about The Who is the way they smashed through every door in the uncharted hallway of rock 'n' roll without leaving much more than some debris for the rest of us to lay claim to."**

Singer Sheryl Crow also sees the importance of The Who:

> **"The Who are just one of those amazing experiences that have not only defied their own hype, they've actually transcended it. They embody everything**

You know you've hit the big time when you appear as yourself on the hit Fox television show *The Simpsons*. In "The Tale of Two Springfields," The Who help Homer reunite the city after a second area code divides the city. A clip from the show can be seen on YouTube.

rock can and should be—rhythm, energy, and the most elusive ingredient of all—passion.**"**

Songs and Synthesizers

When The Who's members looked at the synthesizer, they saw it as something more than a device that could add really cool side effects.

No, it could be "played" like any other instrument. Bands like the Police, Blondie, Boston, and the Cars followed The Who in taking full advantage of the synthesizer.

Most groups cover other musicians' songs once in a while. Musicians as diverse as Green Day, Patti Smith, David Bowie, Pearl Jam, Phish,

The Who continues to perform for many charities and worthy causes. One of those causes is the Teenage Cancer Trust, of which Roger is a long-time supporter. In this photo, Pete is shown performing at a March 2007 concert to benefit the trust. Roger organized the successful concert event.

Van Halen, and the Grateful Dead have covered songs first recorded by The Who. According to some music historians, "My Generation" is perhaps one of the group's most covered songs. Among those who have covered it are Oasis, Patti Smith, Green Day, and Iron Maiden.

On Thursday nights in the United States, millions of television sets are tuned to CBS for *CSI*. Viewers are also getting a dose of The Who; "Who Are You" is the series' theme song.

Some musicians aren't content just covering songs—they cover the band. These tribute bands can be bad, campy, or really good. Some of the most popular Who tribute bands include The Wholigans, Who's Next USA, and the OHM.

Beyond Music

For many years, The Who, individually and as a group, has recognized the need to give back and have participated in charity events. They were front and center for Live Aid and performed at Live 8 as well. They participated in events honoring those who lost their lives as a result of the attacks on New York City's Twin Towers in 2001. They've performed to raise funds for Britain's Teenage Cancer Trust and numerous other worthy causes.

Pete has been involved in many charitable projects on his own. His first solo concert was a benefit to raise money for the Camden Square Play Center. He has been instrumental in providing the space—and funds—for a Meher Baba Center in England. He has been active with the Nordoff-Robbins Music Therapy Foundation, which helps children with autism and developmental disorders. He has also been instrumental in raising funds to help organizations provide drug treatment programs to addicts. In 1979, Pete became the first major rock star to donate his services to Amnesty International.

After John's 2002 death, the John Entwistle Foundation was formed. Though the foundation was established to help music education programs, it has also played a significant role in relief efforts, including helping individuals affected by the 2005 hurricane in Florida. Members of The Who have actively participated in the foundation's projects.

Whether in music or in humanitarian efforts, The Who have been standard-bearers and pioneers. Their legacy will be difficult to surpass.

Late 1950s Roger Daltrey forms the band the Detours.

Late 1950s –1960s Mod culture thrives in Britain.

1960s The British Invasion comes the United States.

1961 Pete Townshend and John Entwistle form the Confederates.

1964 Roger, Pete, John, and Keith form The Who.

"Zoot Suit/I'm the Face" is released under the name the High Numbers.

1965 The Who's first big-selling album, *The Who Sings My Generation*, is released.

"I Can't Explain" becomes the Who's first hit.

1967 The Who plays at the Monterey Pop Festival.

1969 The Who plays at Woodstock.

The rock opera *Tommy* is released.

1971 "Won't Get Fooled" is the first hit single that features the synthesizer.

1975 The film version of *Tommy* is released.

1976 The Who concert at the Charlton Athletic Football Ground is certified as the loudest ever; it holds that distinction for more than ten years.

1978 September 7 Drummer Keith Moon dies.

1979 The film version of *Quadrophenia* is released.

December The Who becomes the third band to appear on the cover of *Time*.

December Eleven fans are killed in a push for seats at a Who concert.

1982 Pete announces that he is an alcoholic; he gets dry.

1983 **December** Pete leaves the group, and The Who disbands.

1985 **July 13** The Who plays at Live Aid.

1988 The Who receives a Lifetime Achievement Award from the British Phonography Industry.

1989 The Who embarks on a reunion tour.

1990 The Who is inducted into the Rock and Roll Hall of Fame.

2000 The BBC broadcasts a form of the Lighthouse project.

2001 The Grammy Awards present The Who with a Lifetime Achievement Award.

October The Who participates in the Concert for New York City.

2002 **June 27** Bassist John Entwistle dies.

September *Q* magazine names The Who one of "50 Bands to See Before You Die."

2005 **July 2** The Who performs at Live 8.

2006 The Who releases its first album in twenty-five years.

October The Who receives the first Freddie Mercury Lifetime Achievement in Live Music Award.

2006–2007 The Who goes on an extended tour.

Albums

1965 *The Who Sings My Generation*

1966 *Happy Jack*

1967 *The Who Sell Out*

1968 *Magic Bus: The Who on Tour*

1969 *Tommy*

1970 *Live at Leeds*

1971 *Meaty Beaty Big and Bouncy*
Who's Next

1973 *Quadrophenia*

1974 *Odds and Sods*

1975 *The Who by Numbers*

1978 *Who Are You*

1979 *The Kids Are Alright*

1981 *Face Dances*
Hooligans

1982 *It's Hard*
Join Together

1983 *Who's Greatest Hits*
Who's Last

1988 *Who's Better, Who's Best*

1990 *Join Together Live*

1994 *Thirty Years of Maximum R&B*

1996 *Live at the Isle of Wight Festival 1970*
My Generation: The Very Best of The Who

1999 *The BBC Sessions*

2000 *Blues to the Bush*

2002 *Encore Series 2002*
The Ultimate Collection

2003 *Live at the Royal Albert Hall*

2004 *Encore Series 2004*
The Who: Then and Now

2006 *Encore Series 2006*
Endless Wire
Live from Toronto

Number-One Single
1981 "You Better You Bet"

Videos
1970 *Live at the Isle of Wight Festival*

1975 *Tommy*

1979 *The Kids Are Alright*
Quadrophenia

1994 *Thirty Years of Maximum R&B Live*

1998 *Roger Daltrey: A Celebration with Pete Townshend
and Music of The Who*

2001 *Live at the Royal Albert Hall*

2004 *Live in Boston*

2005 *Tommy and Quadrophenia Live*

2006 *Live from Toronto*
Quadrophenia
Thunderfingers—John Entwistle—The Who
Tommy Live
The Vegas Job
The Who—Music Box Documentary

Awards and Recognitions
1988 British Phonography Industry: Lifetime Achievement Award.

1990 Inducted into the Rock and Roll Hall of Fame.

1998 VH1: Ranked #9 on the "100 Greatest Artists of Rock 'n' Roll" list.

2000 VH1: Ranked #8 on the "100 Greatest Artists of Hard Rock" list.

2001 Grammy Awards: Lifetime Achievement Award.

2002 Named one of the "50 Bands to See Before You Die" by *Q* magazine.

2006 Recipient: Freddie Mercury Lifetime Achievement in Live
Music Award.

Books

Barnes, Richard. *Who: Maximum R&B*. London: Plexus Publishing, 2004.

Charlesworth, Chris, and Ed Hanel. *The Who: The Complete Guide to Their Music*. London: Omnibus, 2004.

Fletcher, Tony. *Moon: The Life and Death of a Rock Legend*. New York: HarperCollins, 2000.

Marsh, Dave. *Before I Get Old: The Story of the Who*. London: Plexus Publishing, 2003.

McMichael, Joe, and Jack Lyons. *The Who Concert File*. London: Omnibus, 2004.

Neill, Andy, and Matt Kent. *Anyway, Anyhow, Anywhere: The Complete Chronicle of The Who 1958–1978*. London: Virgin Books, 2005.

Web Sites

www.eelpie.com
eelpie.com

www.johnentwistle.com
John Entwistle

www.johnentwistile.org
John Entwistle Foundation

www.petetownshend-whohe.blogspot.com
Pete Townshend

www.rockhall.com
Rock and Roll Hall of Fame

www.thewhotour.com
The Who

acoustic—Used to describe music that is not amplified electronically.

activist—Someone who acts vigorously and sometimes aggressively on behalf of a cause.

amphetamines—A white crystalline compound formerly used as a stimulant of the central nervous system to treat conditions such as depression as well as an appetite suppressor.

angst—A feeling of dread or anxiety.

bootleg—An illegally made product.

covers—New versions of songs made popular by someone else.

demos—A recorded sample of music produced for promotional purposes.

humanitarian—Committed to improving the lives of other people.

infuse—To fill something with strong emotion, enthusiasm, or desire.

mysticism—A system of religious belief or practice that people follow to achieve personal communication or union with the divine.

plight—A difficult or dangerous situation, especially a sad or desperate predicament.

primer—Something that provides basic information.

prolific—Highly productive.

subculture—A separate social group within a larger culture, especially one regarded as existing outside mainstream society.

venues—Locations of events.

Noa Flynn completed graduate studies at the Syracuse University. She lives in New York, where she is a freelance author.

Picture Credits

page

2: Syndication Int'l
8: ZTA/ZOB/WENN
11: UPI Newspictures/David Silpa
12: Mirrorpix
14: Syndication Int'l
17: Popperfoto Archive
18: Brunswick Records/Star Photos
20: Pictorial Press
21: Pictorial Press
23: UPPA/Star Photos
24: Mirrorpix
26: Disc Magazine/Icon Images
29: Mirrorpix

31: MCA Records/Star Photos
33: Columbia Pictures/NMI
34: Polydor Records/Star Photos
36: Polydor Records/Star Photos
38: New Millennium Images
41: Feature Image Archive
42: Warner Bros. Pictures/NMI
44: Mirrorpix
47: Star Photos Archvie
49: John Davisson/Abaca Press
50: Splash News
53: Fox TV/NMI
54: UPI Newspictures

Front cover: Star Photo Archive